Crocheted Amigurumi

COMPILED BY **Amy Palmer**

INTERWEAVE.
interweave.com

*The projects in this collection were
originally published in other Interweave
publications, including* Interweave
Crochet, Interweave Knits, Knitscene,
and Piecework *magazines and*
CrochetMe *eBooks. Some have been
altered to update information and/or
conform to space limitations.*

 Interweave Press LLC,
a division of F+W Media Inc
201 East Fourth Street
Loveland, CO 80537
interweave.com

Printed in the United States
by Versa Press

Table of Contents

Clarence the Monkey
by Brenda K. B. Anderson

Clarence arrived in the office with a simple note: "You know you want me!" Just a little bundle of yarn and some simple stitches bring Clarence's outsize personality to life to charm both children and adults.

Finished Size
About 6½" (16.5 cm) tall.

Yarn
Red Heart Soft Yarn (100% acrylic; 256 yd [234 m]/5 oz [140 g]; ❹): #9344 chocolate (dark brown; MC); #1882 toast (light brown; A); #4420 guacamole (green; B), 1 skein each. Yarn distributed by Coats & Clark.

Hook
Size G/6 (4 mm). Adjust hook size if necessary to obtain correct gauge.

Notions
Polyester fiberfill; two 16 mm safety eyes; stitch marker (m); yarn needle; ½ yd (0.45 m) of any black acrylic worsted-weight yarn for mouth and nostrils.

Gauge
18 sts and 22 rows = 4" (10 cm) in sc.

---

notes

* Clarence is crocheted in a spiral starting at the top of his head, working downward. After changing colors at the waist to make his pants, cont the spiral down the body. Work his left leg first, change colors again, and finish with his left foot. In order to work the right leg, join yarn at the crotch of the pants and work another spiral down the leg ending with the right foot.

* Remember to stuff Clarence (using polyester fiberfill) as you go. After his head and body have been made, stitch on his muzzle, eye area, ears, arms, and tail.

* To change color, work last st of old color to last yo; yo with new color and draw through all lps on hook to complete st. Proceed with new color. Fasten off old color.

Eye Area

With A, ch 12.

ROW 1: Sc in bottom ridge lp of 2nd ch from hook and in each ch across, turn—11 sc.

ROW 2: Ch 1, sk first 2 sc, 7 dc in next sc, sk next 2 sc, sl st in next sc, sk next 2 sc, 7 dc in next sc, sk next sc, sl st in last sc.

Fasten off, leaving a 16" (40.5 cm) tail for sewing. Attach safety eyes at the base of each 7-dc group.

Muzzle

Note: Muzzle is worked from one side to the other (cheek to cheek).

RND 1: With A, make an adjustable lp (see Glossary), 5 sc in ring, pull yarn tail to tighten lp—5 sc.

RND 2: 2 sc in each sc around—10 sc.

RNDS 3–12: Sc in each sc around.

Lightly stuff with polyester fiberfill.

RND 13: [Sc2tog (see Glossary)] 5 times—5 sc.

Fasten off, leaving a 16" (40.5 cm) tail. Using yarn needle, weave tail through flo (see Glossary) of rem 5 sc. Pull tight to close end. Leave yarn tail for sewing.

Ears (make 2)

RND 1: With A, make an adjustable lp, 6 sc in ring, pull tail to tighten lp—6 sc.

RND 2: 2 sc in each sc around—12 sc.

RNDS 3–4: Sc in each sc around.

RND 5: [Sc in next 4 sc, sc2tog] 2 times—10 sc.

Fasten off, leaving a 10" (25.5 cm) tail for sewing. Do not stuff ears.

Arms (make 2)

RND 1: With A, make an adjustable lp, 5 sc in ring, pull tail to tighten lp—5 sc.

RND 2: 2 sc in each sc around—10 sc.

RND 3: Sc in each sc around.

RND 4: [Sc in next 3 sc, sc2tog] 2 times, changing to MC in last st—8 sc.

RNDS 5–8: Sc in each sc around.

RND 9: Sc2tog, sc in next 6 sc—7 sc.

RNDS 10–12: Sc in each sc around.

Fasten off, leaving a 10" (25.5 cm) tail for sewing. Do not stuff arms.

Tail

RND 1: With MC, make an adjustable lp, 5 sc in lp, pull tail to tighten lp.

RNDS 2–13: Sc in each sc around—5 sc.

Fasten off, leaving a 10" (25.5 cm) tail for sewing. Do not stuff tail.

Head, Upper Body, Pants, Legs, and Feet

RND 1: With MC, make an adjustable lp, 6 sc in lp, pull tail to tighten lp—6 sc.

RND 2: 2 sc in each st around—12 sc.

RND 3: [Sc in next sc, 2 sc in next sc] 6 times—18 sc.

RND 4: [Sc in next 2 sc, 2 sc in next sc] 6 times—24 sc.

RND 5: [Sc in next 2 sc, 2 sc in next sc, sc in next sc] 6 times—30 sc.

RND 6: [Sc in next 4 sc, 2 sc in next sc] 6 times—36 sc.

RND 7: [Sc in next sc, 2 sc in next sc, sc in next 7 sc] 4 times—40 sc.

RNDS 8–13: Sc in each sc around.

RND 14: [Sc in next 8 sc, sc2tog] 4 times—36 sc.

RND 15: [Sc in next 3 sc, sc2tog, sc in next sc] 6 times—30 sc.

RND 16: [Sc in next sc, sc2tog, sc in next 2 sc] 6 times—24 sc.

RND 17: [Sc2tog] 12 times—12 sc.

Stuff head with polyester fiberfill.

RND 18: Sc in each sc around.

Upper body

RND 19: 2 sc in each sc around—24 sc.

RND 20: [Sc in next 5 sc, 2 sc in next sc] 4 times—28 sc.

RNDS 21–24: Sc in each sc around, changing to B in last sc of Rnd 24.

Pants

SL ST RND: Sl st in each st around. This rnd is decorative only. Do not work into this rnd of sl sts.

RNDS 25–28: Note: Work behind the sl st rnd and in the sc of Rnd 24. Sc in each sc around.

Divide for legs

RND 29: Ch 2, place marker (pm) in next sc, sk marked sc and next 13 sc, sc in next 14 sc—14 sc and 2 ch.

RND 30: Sc in next 2 ch, sc in next 6 sc, sc2tog, sc in next 6 sts—15 sc.

RND 31: Sc in next 5 sc, sc2tog, sc in next 4 sc, sc2tog, sc in next 2 sc—13 sc.

RND 32: Sc in each sc around.

SL ST RND: Sl st in each st around, changing to MC in last st.

Left foot

RND 33: Working behind sl sts, sc in next 4 sc, 2 sc in each of next 3 sc, sc in next 6 sc—16 sc.

RND 34: Sc in next 4 sc, hdc in next 6 sc, sc in next 6 sc.

RND 35: Sc in each st around, changing to A in last sc.

Bottom of left foot

RND 36: Working in blo (see Glossary), [sc in next 2 sc, sc2tog] 4 times—12 sc.

Stuff upper body, left leg, and foot.

RND 37: [Sc2tog] 6 times—6 sc.

Fasten off, leaving a 6" (15 cm) tail. Using yarn needle, weave tail through flo of rem 6 sc. Pull tight and weave in end.

Right leg

RND 1: Join B with sc in marked sc, sc in next 13 sc, sc in bottom ridge lp of next 2 ch—16 sc.

RND 2: Sc in next 6 sc, sc2tog, sc in next 8 sc—15 sc.

RND 3: Sc in next 2 sc, sc2tog, sc in next 4 sc, sc2tog, sc in next 5 sc—13 sc.

RND 4: Sc in each sc around.

SL ST RND: Sl st in each st around, changing to MC in last st. This rnd is decorative only. Do not work in this rnd of sl sts.

Right foot

RND 5: Working behind sl sts, sc in next 6 sc, 2 sc in next 3 sc, sc in next 4 sc—16 sc.

RND 6: Sc in next 6 sc, hdc in next 6 sc, sc in next 4 sc.

RND 7: Sc in each sc around, changing to A in last st.

Bottom of right foot

RND 8: Working in blo, [sc in next 2 sts, sc2tog] 4 times—12 sc.

Stuff right leg and foot.

RND 9: [Sc2tog] 6 times—6 sc.

Fasten off, leaving a 6" (15 cm) tail. Weave tail through flo of rem 6 sc. Pull tight and weave in end.

Finishing

Sew eye area onto head. Sew muzzle onto head just below lower edge of eye area. Flatten ears and sew to sides of head. Sew tail and arms to body. Use black yarn to make a French knot (see Glossary) for each nostril. Embroider mouth with black yarn by making 2 long stitches. 🖊

BRENDA K. B. ANDERSON makes mascots during the day and lives in a little house in Saint Paul, Minnesota, with her awesome husband and their hairy baby, Mr. Kittypants.

Finished Sizes
Little Livvie stands 2" (5 cm) tall.
Owlivia stands 4½" (11.5 cm) tall.

Yarn
For Little Livvie: Aunt Lydia's Classic Crochet Thread size 10 (100% mercerized cotton; 350 yd [320 m]/3 oz [85 g]; (**0**)): #0131 fudge brown (MC); #0431 pumpkin (CC1); #0420 cream (CC2); 1 ball each.
For Owlivia: Red Heart Soft Yarn (100% acrylic; 256 yd [234 m]/5 oz [140 g]; (**4**)): #9344 chocolate (MC); #4422 tangerine (CC1); #9114 honey (CC2); 1 ball each. Yarns distributed by Coats & Clark.

Hook
For Little Livvie: size 9 (1.15 mm) steel hook.
For Owlivia: size G/6 (4 mm) standard hook. Adjust hook size if necessary to obtain correct gauge.

Notions
For Little Livvie: Polyester fiberfill; embroidery needle; size 8 mm slit pupil safety eyes, sew-on style. **Note:** The washers on most safety eyes are too big to fit behind Little Livvie's face. The stem of the eye has a hole in it for sewing; stitch marker (m; optional).
For Owlivia: Polyester fiberfill; yarn needle; size 15 mm slit pupil safety eyes; stitch marker (m; optional).

Gauge
For Little Livvie: Rnds 1–6 of body = 1¼" (3.2 cm) diameter.
For Owlivia: Rnds 1–6 of body = 2½" (6.5 cm) diameter.

---

notes

* Gauge is not critical for this project. Gauge should be tight enough to make a fabric that will hold the stuffing in place and keep its shape.

* Follow the same instructions to make Little Livvie and Owlivia, using thread for Little Livvie and yarn for Owlivia.

* All pieces (except beak) are worked in spirals. Do not join rnds. Use st marker to indicate beg of rnd, move m up as each rnd is completed. Body is crocheted in spiral down from top of head.

---

stitch guide

Bobble
Yo, insert hook in next st, yo and pull up lp, yo and draw through 2 lps (2 lps on hook), *yo, insert hook in same st, yo and pull up lp, yo and draw through 2 lps; rep from * 4 times (7 lps on hook), yo and draw through all 7 lps.

Owlivia and Little Livvie
by Brenda K. B. Anderson

Owlivia and Little Livvie go simply everywhere together. They are alike in almost every way, though Owlivia is crocheted from worsted-weight yarn and delicate Little Livvie is constructed from crochet thread. This delightful pair presents a great introduction to crocheting amigurumi.

Body

RND 1: With MC, make an adjustable lp (see Glossary), 6 sc in ring (pull yarn tail to close lp)—6 sts.

RND 2: 2 sc in each st around—12 sts.

RND 3: [Sc in next st, 2 sc in next st] 6 times—18 sts.

RND 4: [Sc in next 2 sts, 2 sc in next st] 6 times—24 sts.

RND 5: [Sc in next 3 sts, 2 sc in next st] 6 times—30 sts.

RND 6: [Sc in next 4 sts, 2 sc in next st] 6 times—36 sts.

RND 7: [Sc in next 17 sts, 2 sc in next st] 2 times—38 sts.

RND 8: [Sc in next 6 sts, 2 sc in next st, sc in next 12 sts] 2 times—40 sts.

RNDS 9–15: Sc around.

Shape Back and Tail

RND 16: Sc in next 14 sts, 2 sc in next st, sc in next 4 sts, 2 sc in next st, sc in next 4 sts, 2 sc in next st, sc in next 15 sts—43 sts.

RND 17: Sc in next 17 sts, 2 sc in next st, sc in next 3 sts, 2 sc in next st, sc in next 3 sts, 2 sc in next st, sc in next 17 sts—46 sts.

RND 18: Sc in next 16 sts, 2 sc in next st, sc in next 5 sts, 2 sc in next st, sc in next 6 sts, 2 sc in next st, sc in next 16 sts—49 sts.

RND 19: Sc in next 24 sts, 2 sc in next st, sc in next 24 sts—50 sts.

RND 20: Sc in next 25 sts, 2 sc in next st, sc in next 24 sts—51 sts.

RND 21: Sc in next 25 sts, 2 sc in next st, sc in next 25 sts—52 sts.

RND 22: Sc around.

RND 23: Sc in next 12 sts, [sc2tog (see Glossary), sc in next 4 sts] 2 times, sc2tog 2 times, [sc in next 4 sts, sc2tog] 2 times, sc in next 12 sts—46 sts.

RND 24: Sc in next 10 sts, sc2tog, sc in next 4 sts, sc2tog, sc in next 3 sts, sc2tog 2 times, sc in next 3 sts, sc2tog, sc in next 4 sts, sc2tog, sc in next 10 sts—40 sts.

RND 25: [Sc in next 8 sts, sc2tog] 4 times—36 sts.

RND 26: [Sc in next 2 sts, sc2tog, sc in next 2 sts] 6 times—30 sts.

RND 27: [Sc in next 3 sts, sc2tog] 6 times—24 sts.

RND 28: [Sc2tog, sc in next 2 sts] 6 times—18 sts.

Stuff body firmly with polyester fiber-fill before cont.

RND 29: [Sc in next st, sc2tog] 6 times—12 sts.

RND 30: Sc2tog 6 times—6 sts.

Fasten off leaving a 10" (25.5 cm) tail. Using yarn needle, thread yarn tail through 6 rem sts and pull tight to close hole at bottom. Weave in ends. **Note:** Safety eyes do not attach through body, only through face.

Face

Note: Face is crocheted in a spiral, beg at center with foundation ch.

With CC2, ch 7.

RND 1: 2 sc blo (see Glossary) in 2nd ch from hook, sc blo in next 4 ch, 4 sc in last ch, cont on other side of foundation ch, sc in next 4 ch, 2 sc in last ch—16 sts.

RND 2: *(Sc, hdc) in next st, 2 hdc in next st, sc in next st, sl st in next 2 sts, sc in next st, 2 hdc in next st, (hdc, sc) in next st; rep from *, sl st in first sc to join—24 sts.

Fasten off, leaving a long tail for sewing. Fasten safety eyes through face. If using sew-on eyes, sew them securely through back of face. If using safety eyes with washers, make sure they are securely fastened. Use long tail to sew face onto front of body.

Beak

With CC1, ch 2, 2 sc in 2nd ch from hook.

Fasten off, leaving a 10" (25.5 cm) tail for sewing. Use tail to sew beak onto face using photos for a guide.

Wings (make 2)

Note: Each wing is crocheted in a spiral, starting at the tip and ending at the top edge where it connects to the body.

RND 1: With MC, make an adjustable lp, 6 sc in ring—6 sc.

RND 2: Sc in next 3 sts, 2 sc in next st, sc in last 2 sts—7 sts.

RND 3: Sc in next st, 2 sc in next st, sc in last 5 sts—8 sts.

RND 4: Sc in next 6 sts, 2 sc in next st, sc in last st—9 sts.

RND 5: Sc in next 4 sts, 2 sc in next st, sc in last 4 sts—10 sts.

RND 6: 2 sc in first st, sc in last 9 sts—11 sts.

RND 7: Sc in next 8 sts, 2 sc in next st, sc in last 2 sts—12 sts.

RND 8: Sc in next 5 sts, 2 sc in next st, sc in last 6 sts—13 sts.

RND 9: Sc in next 12 sts, 2 sc in last st—14 sts.

Fold wing flat with working lp at right edge of work. Sl st seam (see Glossary) opening closed. Fasten off, leaving a long tail for sewing. Use tail to sew top edge of wing onto side of body.

Feet (make 2)

Note: Each foot is crocheted in a spiral, starting at heel and ending at toes.

With CC1, rep Rnds 1–9 of wing directions above—14 sts at the end of Rnd 9. Fold foot flat with working lp at right edge of work.

Toe bobbles

Note: Sts seam foot edge closed with toe bobbles and sl sts. With each st, insert hook through 2 sts at a time as foll: Insert hook in through the bottom of foot (from RS to WS) and out through the top of foot (from WS to RS).

ROW 10: Sl st in next st, [bobble (see Stitch Guide) in next st, sl st in next st] 3 times.

Fasten off, leaving a long tail for sewing. Use yarn tail to sew each foot to body.

Weave in ends. 🌿

Frog Charming
by Toni Rexroat

In the story of the Frog Prince, a spoiled princess loses her favorite ball down a well. It is retrieved by a frog prince in exchange for becoming the princess's playmate—to eat with her, play with her, and sleep on her pillow at night. One morning the princess awakens to discover that the frog has been transformed into a handsome prince. Now you can make a frog prince for your own princess.

Finished Size
About 21" (53.5 cm) tall with legs extended.

Yarn
Blue Sky Alpacas Dyed Cotton (100% organically grown cotton; 150 yd [137 m]/3.5 oz [100 g]; (**4**)): #602 honeydew (A), 2 skeins; #613 ink (B), #614 drift (C), #636 jasper (D), and #638 dandelion (E), 1 skein each.

Hook
Size G/6 (4 mm). Adjust hook size if necessary to obtain correct gauge.

Notions
Yarn needle; sewing needle and matching thread; corn-based or polyester stuffing.

Gauge
15 sts and 7 rows = 4" (10 cm) in dc.

notes

* Beg stuffing body, legs, and head just after beg dec.
* Unless otherwise noted, pieces are worked in a spiral without joining each row.

Body

With A, ch 4, sl st in first ch to form ring.

RND 1: Ch 3 (counts as dc), 13 dc in ring, do not join, place marker (pm) in first st to mark beg of rnd—14 dc.

RND 2: 2 dc in each dc around—28 dc.

RND 3: *Dc in next dc, 2 dc in next dc; rep from * around—42 dc.

RND 4: *Dc in next 2 dc, 2 dc in next dc; rep from * around—56 dc.

RNDS 5–10: Dc in each dc around.

RND 11: *Dc in next 2 dc, dc2tog (see Glossary); rep from * around—42 dc.

RND 12: Dc in each st around.

RND 13: *Dc in next dc, dc2tog; rep from * around—28 dc.

RND 14: Dc2tog to m—14 dc.

RND 15: Dc2tog to m, hdc in next st, sc n next st—7 st. Fasten off.

Head

Work as for body through Rnd 4.

RND 5: *Dc in next 3 dc, 2 dc in next dc; rep from * around—70 dc.

Shape mouth

RND 6: Pm in 24th st, *2 dc in next dc, dc in next 2 dc; rep from * to m, move m up, dc to end—78 dc.

RND 7: *Dc2tog, dc in next 2 dc; rep from * to m, dc to end—70 dc.

RND 8: *Dc in next 3 dc, dc2tog; rep from * around—56 dc.

RND 9: *Dc in next 2 dc, dc2tog; rep from * around—42 dc. Stuff head.

RND 10: *Dc in next dc, dc2tog; rep from * around—28 dc.

RND 11: Dc2tog around—14 dc. Fasten off.

Eyes (make 2)

Note: Eyes are worked in joined rnds. With B, ch 4, sl st in first ch to form ring.

RND 1: Ch 2 (counts as dc), 7 dc in ring, sl st in beg ch-2 changing to C in last st—8 dc.

RND 2: Ch 2, dc in first dc, 2 dc in each dc around, sl st in beg ch-2 to join—16 dc.

RND 3: Ch 2, dc in first dc, dc2tog around, sl st in beg ch-2 to join—8 dc. Stuff eye.

RND 4: Ch 2, dc2tog around, sl st in beg ch-2 to join—4 dc. Fasten off.

Arms (make 2)

Hand

With A, ch 10.

RND 1: Dc in 4th ch from hook (3 skipped chs do not count as dc), dc in next 5 ch, 4 dc in last ch, working across back of chain dc in next 5 back ridge lps, 3 dc in last ch, pm in first dc to mark beg of rnd—18 dc.

RND 2: Dc in next 7 dc, dc2tog, dc in next 7 dc, dc2tog—16 dc.

RND 3: Dc2tog, dc in next 4 dc, dc2tog 2 times, dc in next 4 dc, dc2tog—12 dc.

Arm

Dc in each dc until arm measures 7" (18 cm). Stuff arm.

NEXT RND: Dc2tog around.

NEXT RND: Dc2tog to last dc, dc in last dc.

Fasten off, leaving a long tail for sewing.

Legs (make 2)

With A, ch 4, sl st in first ch to form ring.

RND 1: (RS) Ch 3 (counts as dc), 11 dc in ring, do not join, pm in first dc—12 dc.

Work even in dc until leg measures 6½" (16.5 cm), do not fasten off.

Foot

RND 1: *2 dc in next dc, dc in next dc; rep from * around—18 dc.

RND 2: 2 dc in each of next 7 dc, dc in next 11 dc—25 dc. Stuff leg.

RND 3: Dc2tog, 4 dc in next dc, *dc4tog (see Glossary), 4 dc in next dc; rep from *, dc2tog, dc in next 10 dc—26 dc.

RND 4: Dc2tog around—13 dc.

RND 5: Dc2tog to last dc, dc in last dc. Fasten off.

Crown

With E, ch 36, sl st in first ch to form ring.

RNDS 1–2: Ch 2 (counts as dc), dc in each ch around—36 dc.

First point

ROW 1: Ch 2 (counts as first dc), dc in next 4 dc, dc2tog, turn—6 dc.

ROW 2: Ch 2 (does not count as st throughout), dc in next 2 dc, dc2tog—3 dc.

ROW 3: Ch 2, dc2tog. Fasten off.

Next point

*With RS facing, sk next 2 dc, join in next dc.

ROW 1: Ch 2 (counts as first dc), dc in next 4 dc—6 dc.

ROW 2: Ch 2 (does not count as st throughout), dc in next 2 dc, dc2tog—3 dc.

ROW 3: Ch 2, dc2tog. Fasten off.

Rep from * 2 times.

Bowtie

With D, ch 8, sc in 2nd ch from hook and each ch across, turn.

ROWS 1–12: Ch 1, sc across—7 sc.

Middle wrap

Ch 4, sc in 2nd ch from hook and each ch across—3 sc. Rep last row 6 times.

Wrap middle wrap around bowtie and sl st ends tog.

Neck band

With D, ch 4.

NEXT ROW: Sc in 2nd ch from hook and each ch across—3 sc. Rep last row to length needed to wrap around frog's neck. Sew bowtie to neck band.

Ball

With D, ch 4, sl st in first ch to form ring.

RND 1: Ch 2 (counts as dc), 7 dc in ring, pm in first dc to mark beg of rnd—8 dc.

RND 2: 2 dc in each dc around—16 dc.

RND 3: *Dc in next dc, 2 dc in next dc; rep from * around—24 dc.

RND 4: *Dc in next 2 dc, 2 dc in next dc; rep from * around changing to E in last dc—32 dc.

RNDS 5–6: Dc around changing to D in last st of Rnd 6.

RND 7: *Dc in next 2 dc, dc2tog; rep from * around—24 dc. Stuff ball.

RND 8: *Dc in next dc, dc2tog; rep from * around—16 dc.

RND 9: Dc2tog around—8dc.

RND 10: Dc2tog around—4 dc. Fasten off.

Finishing

Using A, sew body to head. Using sewing thread, sew eyes to head and limbs to body. Using B and backstitch (see Glossary), embroider mouth. Position bowtie around neck and sew ends tog. Weave in loose ends. 🍃

TONI REXROAT is the editor of CrochetMe.com. When not working, she is busy dreaming of ways to make fairy tales come to life.

BFF Finger Puppets
by Marcy Smith

Perfect your crochet and knitting skills with these small friends from *Interweave Crochet* editor Marcy Smith. Pinki's crocheted dress and matching hat complement Blu's dress and festive hair ribbons.

Finished Size
3¾" (9.5 cm) tall.

Yarn
Spud & Chloë Fine (80% superwash wool, 20% silk, 248 yd [227 m]/2.25 oz [65 g]): #7808 sassafras (pink; A), #7803 dachshund (brown; B), #7800 popcorn (white; C), and #7805 anemone (blue; D), 1 skein each. Yarn distributed by Blue Sky Alpacas.

Hooks and Needles
Pinki: Size C/2 (2.75 mm) crochet hook; **Blu:** Size D/3 (3.25 mm): double-pointed needles (dpn) and size C/2 (2.75 mm) crochet hook. Adjust needle or hook size if necessary to obtain the correct gauge.

Notions
Markers (m); tapestry needle; small amount of fiberfill.

Gauge
32 sts and 40 rows = 4" (10 cm) in St st on needles; 28 sts and 24 rows = 4" (10 cm) in sc.

-----

notes

* Pinki is crocheted and Blu is knitted.

* Both dolls are worked in one piece from the hem of the dress to the top of the head. Pinki's arms are worked from a slip-stitch join to the body; Blu's arms are worked separately in I-cord and attached. The edge of Blu's dress has a crocheted border to help the hem lie flat. To make her completely knitted, work three rows of garter stitch at the beginning of the dress, in MC or CC. To do this, purl one round, knit one round, purl one round, then resume; knit one row with MC before working decrease row.

* See Glossary for all crochet terms.

-----

stitch guide

Increase in single crochet (inc in sc)
Sc in next st, sc again in same st—1 st inc'd.

Pinki

Note: Doll is worked from the R3, do not turn. For dress portion, join each rnd with a sl st in first st; this prevents a color jog in the stripes. Work the head in a spiral without joining. For both methods, mark the first st with a removable marker.

Dress

With A, ch 30, join with sl st in first ch, being careful not to twist chains.

RND 1: Ch 1, sc in each ch around (30 sc), join with sl st in first sc, pulling B through sl st.

RND 2: With B, *sc in each of next 4 sts, sc2tog (see Glossary); rep from * around, join with sl st in first sc, pulling A through sl st—25 sc rem.

RND 3: With A, sc in each sc around, join with sl st in first st, pulling B through sl st.

RND 4: With B, *sc in each of next 3 sts, sc2tog; rep from * around, join with sl st in first sc, pulling A through sl st—20 sc rem.

RND 5: With A, sc in each sc around, join with sl st in first st, pulling B through sl st.

RND 6: With B, *sc in each of next 3 sts, sc2tog; rep from * around, join with sl st in first sc, pulling A through sl st—16 sc rem.

RNDS 7–13: With A, sc in each sc around, join with sl st in first st.

RND 14: Sc2tog around, joining C in sl st—8 sc rem.

RND 15: With C, sc in each sc around.

RND 16: 2 sc in each sc around—16 sc.

RND 17: Sc in each sc around.

RND 18: *Sc in next sc, inc in sc (see Stitch Guide); rep from * around—24 sc.

RNDS 19–23: Sc in each sc around

RND 24: *Sc in next sc, sc2tog; rep from * around—16 sc rem.

RND 25: Sc in each sc around.

RND 26: Sc2tog around—8 sc rem.

RND 27: Sc2tog around—4 sc rem.

Cut yarn. Fasten off. Thread tail on tapestry needle and use to draw top of head tog. Stuff head with fiberfill through neck opening. With D, embroider eyes with satin st (see Glossary). With A, embroider mouth with backstitch (see Glossary).

Arms

Join A with sl st on side of body about 4 rows down from neck. Ch 13, turn, sl st in 2nd ch from hook and each ch across. Cut yarn and fasten off.

Thread yarn ends on tapestry needle and pull to inside. Tie ends tog and clip. Rep for other arm.

Hair

Cut 25–30 strands of B and about 6 strands of A each 12" (30.5 cm) long (or desired length). Fold a yarn strand in half, use hook to pull loop under a st on head; pull both ends through loop and tighten. Rep with rem strands to fill in hair.

Hat

With A, ch 24. Join with sl st to first chain, being careful not to twist.

RNDS 1–3: Sc in each sc around.

Press hat tog so front and back are flat, sl st across top of hat, matching front and back sts (12 sl st). Cut yarn. Place hat on doll and use yarn ends to tack hat down.

Blu

Dress

With D, CO 45 sts. Distribute evenly over 3 dpn, place marker (pm), and join in the rnd.

RNDS 1–3: Knit.

RND 4: *K3, k2tog (see Glossary); rep from * around— 36 sts rem.

RNDS 5–6: Knit.

RND 7: *K2, k2tog; rep from * around—27 sts rem.

RND 8: Knit.

RND 9: *K1, k2tog; rep from * around—18 sts rem.

RNDS 10–19: Knit.

RND 20: [K2tog] around—9 sts rem.

RND 21: With D, knit.

RND 22: K1f&b (see Glossary) in each st around—18 sts.

RND 23: Knit.

RND 24: *K1, k1f&b; rep from * around—27 sts.

RNDS 25–31: Knit.

RND 32: *K1, k2tog; rep from * around—18 sts rem.

RND 33: *K1, k2tog; rep from * around—12 sts rem.

RND 34: [K2tog] around—6 sts rem.

Cut yarn. Thread tail on tapestry needle, run through rem 6 sts, and cinch to close. Stuff head with fiberfill through neck opening. With D, embroider eyes with satin st (see Glossary). With A, embroider mouth with backstitch (see Glossary).

Arms (make 2)

CO 2 sts. Work 12-row I-cord (see Glossary).

NEXT RND: K2tog. Fasten off rem st.

Weave beg tail through arm. Thread yarn ends through body at arm placement (see photo) and tie ends tog.

Hair

Cut about 15 strands of B and D each 6" (15 cm) long (or desired length). Thread a strand of B and D tog on tapestry needle. Insert needle under st on head and pull yarn halfway through. Remove needle. Tie yarns into square knot, snug against head. Rep with rem hair, filling in as desired.

Dress trim

With hook, join A at hem with sl st. Work sc in joining st, *ch 1, sk 1 knit st, sc in next st; rep from * around, end with sc in final st, sl st in first sc. Cut yarn and fasten off. Weave in ends.

Waist trim

Cut a 6" (15 cm) strand of A, weave over and under sts at waist. Pull ends to inside and tie off. 🌿

MARCY SMITH is the editor of *Interweave Crochet*. You may be familiar with Wimi, her small knitted companion, who has been featured in newspaper columns and craft blogs alike.

Tree-garumi
by Vickie Howell

In my house the kids are way hip to amigurumi. If it's small and cute, they want it. This project combines a cute trend with a nod to nature. I bring you Tree-garumi!

VICKIE HOWELL is a mother, designer, writer, viral-marketing consultant, and spokesperson for Caron International Yarns. Sheep(ish), the first yarn under her co-branded line with Caron, is available in stores and online. For information, visit www.vickiehowell.com.

Finished Size
4½" (11.5 cm) tall.

Yarn
Caron Sheep(ish) (70% acrylic, 30% wool; 167 yds [153 m]/3 oz [85 g]; (**4**)): chartreuse(ish) (MC), espresso(ish) (CC), 1 ball each.

Hook Size
H/8 (5 mm) hook. Adjust hook size if necessary to obtain correct gauge.

Notions
Yarn needle; small amount of stuffing.

Body

With MC, ch 28, sl st in first ch to form ring.

RND 1: Ch 1, sc in each ch around, sl st in first sc to join—28 sc.

RNDS 2–3: Ch 1, sc around, sl st in first sc to join.

RND 4: Ch 1, [sc in next 2 sc, sc2tog] around, sl st in first sc to join—21 sc.

RNDS 5–7: Rep Rnd 2.

RND 8: Ch 1, [sc2tog, sc in next sc] around, sl st in first sc to join—14 sc.

RND 9: Rep Rnd 2.

RND 10: Ch 1, sc2tog around, sl st in first sc to join—7 sc.

RND 11: Rep Rnd 2.

RND 12: Sc2tog 3 times, sc—4 sc. Fasten off.

Base

With MC, make an adjustable lp (see Glossary), 6 sc in ring, sl st in first sc to join.

RND 1: Ch 1, 2 sc in each sc around, sl st in first sc to join—12 sc.

RND 2: Ch 1, [2 sc in next sc, sc in next sc] around, sl st in first sc to join—18 sc.

RND 3: Ch 1, [2 sc in next sc, sc in next 2 sc] around, sl st in first sc to join—24 sc.

RND 4: Ch 1, [2 sc in next sc, sc in next 3 sc] around, sl st in first sc to join—30 sc. Fasten off, leaving a 12" (30.5 cm) tail for sewing.

Trunk

With CC, make an adjustable lp (see Glossary), 6 sc in ring, do not join.

RND 1: 2 sc in each sc around—12 sc.

RND 2: Sc around.

Cont in spiral rnds to desired length. Fasten off, leaving a 6" (15 cm) tail for sewing.

Finishing

Stuff tree body and trunk with fiberfill. Sew base to trunk and tree to base. Weave in ends. 🌿

Crochet a Lamb

by Meg Grossman

The combination of fine yarn for the lamb's legs, underside, and face, with fuzzy yarn for the fleece, is particularly intriguing. The body of the lamb is an armature over which the crocheted fleece is sewn.

Finished Size

10" (25.5 cm) from nose to beginning of tail, about 5¾" (14.5 cm) tall.

Yarn

Fingering- or baby-weight yarn, 1.75 oz [50 g]; (❷): natural, sportweight yarn with soft fuzzy texture; 1.75 oz [50 g]; (❷): natural, embroidery floss for mouth and nostrils, red.

Hook

D/3 (3.25 mm) for fingering yarn, size F/5 (3.75 mm) for sportweight yarn.

Notions

Yarn needle; embroidery needle; sewing thread to match yarn; 1 yd cotton batting; 1 yd heavy-duty nonfusible interfacing; 2 black beads for eyes; ribbon for neck.

Gauge

11 sts = 2" (5 cm) with fingering yarn and size D/3 hook; 3 sts = 1" (2.5 cm) with sportweight yarn and size 5 hook over dc.

---

notes

* *Fasten off:* break yarn, draw end through lp on hook, tighten. *Join:* attach to start of rnd with a sl st. *Work even:* work into previous row or rnd without inc or dec.

* Weave in yarn at the beg of the ears only; end yarn will be used to sew the ears to the head. Rem yarn ends will not show on the inside of the work.

Front Legs (make 2)

RND 1: With fingering yarn and size D/3 hook, ch 4, join (see Notes); ch 2, 10 dc in ring; join.

RND 2: Ch 2, dc around, working 2 dc in every second st; join.

RND 3: Ch 2, dec for top of foot as follows: * dc in first st, dc2tog (see Glossary); rep from * around; join.

RNDS 4–9: Work even in dc.

RND 10: Ch 2, * dc in next 4 sts, 2 dc in next dc; rep from * around, join.

RND 11: Work even.

RND 12: Ch 2, * dc in next 3 sts, 2 dc in next dc; rep from * 2 times. Fasten off.

Back Legs (make 2)

Work as for front legs through Rnd 9.

RND 10: Ch 2, 2 dc in next dc; dc in next st; rep from * until 4 sts rem, dc in last 4 sts.

RND 11: Work even.

RND 12: Ch 2, dc in first 2 sts, 2 dc in next dc, dc in next dc, 2 dc in next dc, dc in last 8 sts; join, fasten off.

Body

ROW 1: With fingering yarn and size D/3 hook, ch 21, dc in 3rd ch from hook and in each rem ch across; turn.

ROWS 2–16: Ch 2, work even in dc; turn.

ROW 17: Sl st in first 5 sts, ch 2, work 9 dc; turn, leaving rem sts unworked.

ROW 18: Ch 2, dc in each st across; fasten off.

NEXT ROW: Rotate body piece so Row 1 is at the top of the work. With right side facing, skip first 5 sts, join yarn in next st, ch 2, dc in next 9 sts; turn.

FOLLOWING 2 ROWS: Work even. Fasten off.

Head

RND 1: Ch 2, 4 dc in 2nd ch from hook; join.

RND 2: Ch 2, 2 dc in each st a round; join.

RNDS 3–9: Ch 2, dc around, inc twice in each rnd; join.

Fasten off at end of Rnd 9.

Ears (make 2)

ROW 1: Ch 9, skip 3 ch, tr in 6 rem ch; turn.

ROW 2: Ch 2, dc in next 4 sts, 5 dc in ch-3 tch of Row 1, 5 dc along other side of tr worked in foundation ch; turn.

ROW 3: Ch 2, dc in next 4 sts, 2 dc in next st, dc in next st, 3 dc next st, 2 dc next st, 2 dc in next st, dc in rem sts. Break yarn, leaving long tail to sew the ear to the head; fasten off.

Fleece

Change to the sportweight yarn and size F/5 hook for fleece and tail.

RND 1: Beg at the head and neck area, ch 15, join. Ch 3, 2 tr in each ch; join.

RNDS 2–3: Ch 3, work even in tr; join.

RNDS 4–6: Ch 2, work even in dc; join; fasten off.

Flap for the back

Join yarn and work tr back and forth over center 22 sts of last rnd of fleece for 9 rows or until fleece is as long as the body. Fold the last row in half and sl st the edges together up to the fold. Fasten off.

Tail

ROW 1: Ch 17, sk 3 ch, tr in rem 14 ch across. Turn.

ROWS 2–4: Ch 3, tr in each st across; turn. Fasten off at the end of last row.

Finish the tail

Fold the strip lengthwise and sl st together. The tail should curve because tr edge is much looser than ch edge. Break yarn, leaving long tail to sew the tail to the body. Fasten off.

Armature

Crumple pieces of the cotton batting to roughly the size of the body. Wrap them in another piece of batting and lash with yarn to hold in place. Shape and bind down one end for the head. Form the pairs of legs by rolling up a rectangle of interfacing and batting together and wrapping tightly with yarn.

Put the legs in place on the body by threading them through the lashing on the body mass. Make sure the body is the right size by trying on all the crocheted parts.

Clip, trim, and lash tighter or looser until the shape is correct. Thread a double length of sewing thread into the embroidery needle and stitch the legs to the body.

Dressing the Lamb

Once all the crocheted parts are on the body, thread the tapestry needle with a length of the fingering yarn. Beginning where one of the legs meets the fleece and underside, join the pieces tog with a loose overcast stitch. Push any loose ends of yarn to the inside as you stitch past them.

To attach the ears and tail, thread the yarn ends into the tapestry needle and stitch down. Using the embroidery needle and sewing thread, anchor the ears in place to the cotton batting of the body. Sew on the beads for the eyes. Using the embroidery floss, stitch in the mouth and nostrils. Tie the ribbon around the lamb's neck. The little baby is ready to be adopted—if you can give it up! 🌿

MEG GROSSMAN, lead interpreter for textiles at Old Sturbridge Village in Sturbridge, Massachusetts, has been teaching textile classes and workshops since 1985. She earned her BFA in crafts/textiles at the University of the Arts in Philadelphia, Pennsylvania.

Finished Size
6½" (16.5 cm) tall.

Yarn
Cascade 220 (100% Peruvian highland wool; 220 yd [200 m]/3.5 oz [100 g]; (4)), #9478 (pink; MC), #7808 (purple; CC1), #8909 (fuchsia; CC2), #8509 (gray; CC3), 1 hank each.

Hook
Size E/4 (3.5 mm) Adjust hook size if necessary to obtain correct gauge.

Notions
White felt; st marker (m); two 9 mm black safety eyes; sewing needle and white thread; black embroidery floss; polyester fiberfill; craft glue.

Gauge
Gauge is not critical for this project.

notes

* Exact gauge is not necessary for this project. Gauge should be tight enough to make a fabric that will hold the stuffing in place and keep its shape.
* All pieces are worked in spirals. Do not join rnds. Use st marker (m) to indicate beg of rnd, move m up as each rnd is completed.
* To change color, work last st of old color to last yo. Yo with new color and draw through all lps on hook. Proceed with new color. Fasten off old color.
* Body is worked through Rnd 36, then eyes are made before cont body. This is for ease in attaching safety eyes.

stitch guide

Bobble
Yo, insert hook in indicated st and pull up lp (3 lps on hook), [yo, insert hook in same st and pull up lp] 2 times (7 lps on hook), yo and draw through all 7 lps on hook.

Lovey the Lovely
by Allison Hoffman

Lovey was born on Valentine's Day. She knew she was a little different, what with the horns and all, but with beautiful girly stripes, she decided to embrace her monstrous good looks and adorn her graceful horns with a tiny flower. She smiled, batted her eyelashes, and I took her picture.

Body

RND 1: With MC, make an adjustable lp (see Glossary), 6 sc in lp—6 sc.

RND 2: 2 sc in each st around—12 sc.

RND 3: [2 sc in next st, sc in next st] 6 times—18 sc.

RND 4: [2 sc in next st, sc in next 2 sts] 6 times—24 sc.

RND 5: [2 sc in next st, sc in next 3 sts] 6 times—30 sc.

RND 6: [2 sc in next st, sc in next 4 sts] 6 times—36 sc.

RND 7: [2 sc in next st, sc in next 5 sts] 6 times—42 sc.

RNDS 8–14: Sc around, change to CC1 in last st.

RNDS 15–17: Sc around, change to CC2 in last st.

RND 18: Sc around.

RND 19: [Sc2tog, sc in next 5 sts] 6 times—36 sc.

RNDS 20–21: Sc around.

RND 22: [Sc2tog, sc in next 4 sts] 6 times, change to MC in last st—30 sc.

RNDS 23–24: Sc around, change to CC1 in last st.

RND 25: Sc around, change to CC2 in last st.

RND 26: Sc around.

RND 27: [Sc2tog, sc in next 3 sts] 6 times—24 sc.

RND 28: Sc around, change to MC in last st.

RND 29: Sc around, change to CC1 in last st.

RND 30: Sc around.

Shape leg

RND 31: Sc in next 12 sts, sk next 12 sts—12 sc.

RND 32: Beg at first st of Rnd 31, sc around, change to CC2 in last st.

RNDS 33–34: Sc around, change to MC in last st.

RND 35: Sc in next 7 sts, 3 hdc in next st, hdc in next 3 sts, 3 hdc in next st—16 sts.

RND 36: Sc in next 8 sts, [bobble (see Stitch Guide) in next st (for toe), sl st in next st] 3 times, sc in next 2 sts. Fasten off.

Eyes (make 2)

Cut 2 ovals from white felt. Cut tiny slits in center of felt and insert one safety eye into each oval. Attach safety eyes to face. Sew edges of white felt down with white thread. With black embroidery floss, embroider straight st (see Glossary) eyelashes, using photograph on page 15 as a guide. Stuff body.

Second Leg

RND 1: Join CC1 with sc in first skipped st of Rnd 30, sc in each rem skipped st around—12 sc.

RNDS 2–4: Rep Rnds 32–34 of shape leg to form other leg.

RND 5: Sc in next 2 sts, 3 hdc in next st, hdc in next 3 sts, 3 hdc in next st, sc in next 5 sts—16 sts.

RND 6: Sc in next 4 sts, [bobble in next st, sl st in next st] 3 times, sc in next 6 sts. Fasten off.

Soles of Feet (make 2)

RND 1: With MC, ch 4, sc in bottom ridge lp of 2nd ch from hook and in next ch, 3 hdc in next ch, rotate to work across other side of ch, sc in next 2 ch, sc in beg ch; do not join—8 sts.

RND 2: Sc in next 2 sts, 3 hdc in next st, hdc in next st, 3 hdc in next st, sc in next 3 sts—12 sts.

RND 3: Sc in next 3 sts, 3 hdc in next st, hdc in next 3 sts, 3 hdc in next st, sc in next 4 sts—16 sts. Fasten off, leaving a long tail for sewing.

Stuff legs firmly. Sew soles of feet to bottom of each leg, making them a little flat so monster will stand.

Arms (make 2)

RND 1: Beg at hand, with CC2, make an adjustable lp, 6 sc in lp—6 sc.

RND 2: 2 sc in each st around—12 sc.

RNDS 3–5: Sc around, change to CC1 in last st.

RND 6: Sc in next 5 sts, bobble in next st, sc in next 6 sts.

RNDS 7–8: Sc around, change to MC in last st.

RNDS 9–10: Sc around, change to CC2 in last st.

RND 11: Sc in next 5 sts, sc2tog, sc in next 5 sts, change to CC2 in last st—11 sc.

RND 12: Sc around.

RND 13: Sc in next 2 sts, sc2tog, sc in next 7 sts—10 sc.

RNDS 14–15: Sc around, change to MC in last st.

RNDS 16–17: Sc around, change to CC2 in last st.

RNDS 18–20: Sc around, change to CC2 in last st.

RND 21: Sc in next 4 sts, sc2tog, sc in next 4 sts—9 sc.

RND 22: Sc around, change to MC in last st.

RNDS 23–25: Sc around, change to CC2 in last st.

RND 26: Sc in next 3 sts, sc2tog, sc in next 4 sts—8 sc.

Fasten off, leaving a long tail for sewing. Stuff arm firmly. Thread tail through sts of last rnd and pull to close opening. Sew arm to body.

Horns (make 2)

RND 1: With CC3, make an adjustable lp, 3 sc in lp—3 sc.

RND 2: 2 sc in each st around—6 sc.

RNDS 3–4: Sc around.

RND 5: [2 sc in next st, sc in next st] 3 times—9 sc.

RND 6–7: Sc in next 3 sts, hdc in next 3 sts, sc in next 3 sts.

Fasten off, leaving a long tail for sewing. Stuff and sew to head.

Mouth

Using 6 strands of black embroidery floss, embroider a wide smile across face. Cut small triangle from white felt (for tooth) and glue to mouth.

Flower

RND 1: With CC2, make an adjustable lp, 9 sc in lp, sl st in first sc to join.

RND 2: *Ch 1, (dc, hdc) in next st, sl st in next st; rep from * around, working last sl st in joining sl st.

Fasten off, leaving a long tail. Sew onto head near one horn. 🍃

ALLISON HOFFMAN is an amigurumi designer who is inspired by pop culture and her three little boys. She loves creating quirky toys with a sense of humor. She blogs at www.craftyiscool.blogspot.com.

Ellie the Giraffe

by Gina Reneé Padilla

I would like to introduce you to Ellie the Giraffe, who stands at a staggering 8½" (21.5 cm) tall. Ellie loves long walks across the African plains and is looking for someone to love her.

Finished Size
8½" (21.5 cm) tall.

Yarn
Lion Brand Vanna's Choice (100% acrylic; 170 yd [156 m]/3.5 oz [100 g]; (4)): #860-127 espresso (dark brown; MC), 1 ball.

Lion Brand Vanna's Choice Baby (100% acrylic; 170 yd [156 m]/3.5 oz [100 g]; (4)): #840-157 duckie (soft yellow; CC), 1 ball.

Hook
Size G/6 (4 mm). Adjust hook size if necessary to obtain correct gauge.

Notions
Stitch markers (m); yarn needle; two 9 mm black safety eyes; polyester fiberfill.

Gauge
14 sts and 16 rows = 4" (10 cm) in sc. Gauge is not critical for this project.

---

notes

---

* Exact gauge is not critical for this project. Gauge should be tight enough to make a fabric that will hold the stuffing in place and keep its shape.

* All pieces are worked in spirals. Do not join rnds. Use st marker (m) to indicate beg of rnd and move m up as each rnd is completed.

* To change color, work last st of old color to last yo. Yo with new color and draw through all lps on hook. Proceed with new color. Fasten off old color.

Head

RND 1: With MC, make an adjustable lp (see Glossary), 6 sc in ring—6 sts.

RND 2: 2 sc in each st around (see Notes)—12 sts.

RND 3: [2 sc in next st, sc in next st] 6 times—18 sts.

RND 4: Sc in next 3 sts, 2 sc in each of next 3 sts, sc in next 6 sts, 2 sc in each of next 3 sts, sc in next 3 sts—24 sts.

RNDS 5–8: Sc around.

Shape nose

RND 9: [Sc2tog (see Glossary), sc in next 2 sts] 6 times—18 sts.

RND 10: [Sc2tog, sc in next st] 6 times—12 sts.

RND 11: [2 sc in next sc, sc in next st] 6 times—18 sts.

RNDS 12–15: Sc around.

Using picture as a guide, attach safety eyes bet Rnds 12 and 13. Beg stuffing with fiberfill. Cont to stuff as needed until head is complete.

RND 16: [Sc2tog, sc in next st] 6 times—12 sts.

RND 17: [Sc2tog] 6 times—6 sts.

Fasten off, leaving a long tail. Use tail to sew opening closed. Weave in ends.

Body

RNDS 1–3: With A, work Rnds 1–3 of head—18 sts.

RND 4: [2 sc in next st, sc in next 2 sts] 6 times—24 sts.

RND 5: [2 sc in next st, sc in next 3 sts] 6 times—30 sts.

RNDS 6–18: Sc around.

RND 19: [Sc2tog, sc in next 3 sts] 6 times—24 sts.

RND 20: [Sc2tog, sc in next 2 sts] 6 times—18 sts.

Beg stuffing with fiberfill. Cont to stuff as needed until body is complete.

RND 21: [Sc2tog, sc in next st] 6 times—12 sts.

RND 22: Sc2tog 6 times—6 sts. Fasten off, leaving a long tail. Use tail to sew opening closed.

Legs (make 4)

RNDS 1–3: With CC, work Rnds 1–3 of head—18 sts.

RNDS 4–5: Sc around.

RND 6: [Sc2tog, sc in next st] 6 times, changing to MC in last st—12 sts. Fasten off CC.

RNDS 7–14: Sc around.

Stuff legs. Fasten off, leaving a long tail for sewing. Sew all 4 legs to underside of body.

Neck

With A, ch 14, sl st in first ch to form ring.

RND 1: Sc in each ch around—14 sc.

RND 2: Sc around.

Rep last rnd until neck measures 2¼" (5.5 cm) from beg. Sew one end of neck tube to top of one end of body. Stuff with fiberfill. Sew head to other end of tube. Using picture as a guide, bend head down and sew to neck.

Ears (make 2)

With MC, ch 2, 6 sc in 2nd ch from hook. Fasten off, leaving a long tail for sewing. Using picture as a guide, sew ears to head.

Horns (make 2)

With CC, ch 2, 3 sc in 2nd ch from hook. Fasten off, leaving a long tail for sewing. Using picture as a guide, sew horns to head between ears.

Tail

Cut three 10" (25.5 cm) strands of MC. Pull strands through st where you want the tail. Braid strands, then knot tail at end of braid. Trim end of tail.

Spots (make as many as desired)

RND 1: With CC, make an adjustable lp, 6 sc in ring—6 sts.

Larger spot only

RND 2: 2 sc in each st around—12 sts.

Fasten off, leaving a long tail for sewing.

Finishing

Arrange spots as desired and sew to giraffe. 🖋

GINA RENEÉ PADILLA is a stay-at-home wife and mom to seven children. She is a very crafty person, thanks to her mom, Barbara, and a self-taught knitter and crocheter. She enjoys creating new patterns and stuffed toys for her Etsy shop.

Finished Size
6" (15 cm) tall and 5½" (14 cm) wide at ears.

Yarn
Lion Brand Vanna's Choice (100% acrylic; 170 yd [156 m]/3.5 oz [100 g]; (4)): #124 toffee (brown; MC), 1 ball and #149 silver grey (MC), 1 ball.

Caron International Yarn Simply Soft Brites (100% acrylic; 366 yd [334 m]/7 oz [198 g]; (4)): #9606 lemonade (yellow; CC), 1 skein.

Hook
Size F/5 (3.75 mm). Adjust hook size if necessary to obtain correct gauge.

Notions
Yarn needle; stitch marker (m); white sewing thread; white sewing needle; one 9" × 12" (23 × 30.5 cm) sheet of felt in white; small pieces of felt in brown, black, and pink; 1 pair of 15 mm solid black safety eyes; black crochet thread or embroidery floss; craft glue; polyester fiberfill; two 3¾" (9.5 cm) pieces of flexible twist tie.

Gauge
20 sts and 16 rows = 4" (10 cm) in sc. Gauge is not critical for this project.

----

notes
* Exact gauge is not necessary for this project. Gauge should be tight enough to make a fabric that will hold the stuffing in place and keep its shape.
* All pieces are worked in spirals. Do not join rnds. Use st marker (m) to indicate beg of rnd and move m up as each rnd is completed.

Ayo
Head
RND 1: Beg at top of head, with MC, ch 2, 6 sc in 2nd ch from hook—6 sts.

RND 2: 2 sc in each st around—12 sts.

RND 3: [Sc in next st, 2 sc in next st] 6 times—18 sts.

RND 4: [Sc in next 2 sts, 2 sc in next st] 6 times—24 sts.

RND 5: [Sc in next 3 sts, 2 sc in next st] 6 times—30 sts.

RND 6: [Sc in next 4 sts, 2 sc in next st] 6 times—36 sts.

RND 7: [Sc in next 5 sts, 2 sc in next st] 6 times—42 sts.

RNDS 8–14: Sc around.

Ayo & Kiki the Monkeys
by Joanna Ma

Ayo, which means "happiness" in Nigerian, spreads warmth and laughter with his cute waving arm and invitingly curly tail. With ears like coconut shells, large tapioca eyes, and sweet bananas resting atop his head, Ayo is the perfect monkey companion on any blue Monday. Kiki grew up in a zoo after she was found sitting on a swing in a playground all by herself. No one knows how she got there, but no one doubts her playful nature! Entertaining guests at the zoo is a tough job, but Kiki has discovered just the trick to challenge herself while exciting zoo-goers. She cleverly balances bananas on her head, a skill she learned from watching the seals balance balls on their nose at a show her zookeeper took her to.

RND 15: [Sc in next 5 sts, sc2tog (see Glossary)] 6 times—36 sts.

RND 16: [Sc in next 4 sts, sc2tog] 6 times—30 sts.

RND 17: [Sc in next 3 sts, sc2tog] 6 times—24 sts.

RND 18: [Sc in next 2 sts, sc2tog] 6 times—18 sts.

Fasten off, leaving a long tail for sewing.

Face

From white felt, cut face shape. Cut slits in felt where you would like to place eyes. From black felt, cut a small oval for nose. Glue nose centered below eyes. With black embroidery floss, embroider mouth just below nose. From pink felt, cut small circles and glue to face for cheeks. Place face on head, one rnd above last rnd (Rnd 17). Insert and fasten eyes into slits and through head. With sewing needle and white thread, sew face to head. Stuff head firmly with polyester fiberfill.

Body

RNDS 1–6: Beg at bottom of body, with MC, work Rnds 1–6 of head—36 sts.

RNDS 7–8: Sc around.

RND 9: [Sc in next 4 sts, sc2tog] 6 times—30 sts.

RND 10: Sc around.

RND 11: [Sc in next 3 sts, sc2tog] 6 times—24 sts.

RND 12: Sc around.

RND 13: [Sc in next 2 sts, sc2tog] 6 times—18 sts.

Fasten off.

From white felt, cut heart-shaped chest piece. With sewing needle and white thread, sew chest piece to body, one row below top of body. Stuff firmly.

Ears (make 2)

RNDS 1–6: With MC, work Rnds 1–6 of head—36 sts.

Fasten off, leaving a long tail for sewing. Do not stuff ears.

Arms (make 2)

RND 1: With MC, ch 2, 4 sc in 2nd ch from hook—4 sts.

RND 2: 2 sc in each st around—8 sts.

RNDS 3–8: Sc around.

RND 9: Sc in next 4 sts, sl st in next st, leave rem sts unworked—4 sts.

Fasten off, leaving a long tail for sewing. Do not stuff arms.

Feet (make 2)

RNDS 1–2: Work Rnds 1–2 of head—12 sts.

RNDS 3–4: Sc around.

Stuff firmly. Fasten off, leaving a long tail for sewing.

Tail

RND 1: With MC, ch 2, 6 sc in 2nd ch from hook—6 sts.

RNDS 2–7: Sc around.

RND 8: Sc in next 4 sts, sc2tog—5 sts.

RNDS 9–15: Sc around.

Do not stuff tail. Fasten off, leaving a long tail for sewing. Insert twist tie in tail until it reaches the tip. Trim off any excess tie.

Bananas (make 2)

RND 1: With CC, ch 2, 3 sc in 2nd ch from hook—3 sts.

RND 2: 2 sc in each st around—6 sts.

RNDS 3–5: Sc around.

RND 6: Sc in next 4 sts, sc2tog—5 sts.

RNDS 7–8: Sc around.

Fasten off, leaving a long tail for sewing. Do not stuff bananas. Sew bananas tog at open ends, for tops of bananas. From brown felt, cut a small circle for stem. Glue stem over top of bananas.

Finishing

Note: Use long tails to sew pieces tog. Sew head to body. Make sure heart-shaped chest piece is centered directly below face. For ears, fold circles in half to create semicircles. Sew ears to sides of head in cup-like formation. From white felt, cut two semicircle shapes for inner ear pieces. Glue these pieces inside ears. Position arms on sides of body, with one arm reaching upward and the other reaching downward. Sew arms in place. Position feet facing outward from body, ensuring that placement will allow monkey to sit on its own. Sew feet to body. Sew tail to back end of body. Curl tail to your liking once sewn in place. Position bananas anywhere you think is most charming, even on the monkey's tail. Sew bananas in place.

Kiki

Head

RND 1: Beg at top of head, with MC, ch 2, 6 sc in 2nd ch from hook—6 sts.

RND 2: 2 sc in each st around—12 sts.

RND 3: [Sc in next st, 2 sc in next st] 6 times—18 sts.

RND 4: [Sc in next 2 sts, 2 sc in next st] 6 times—24 sts.

RND 5: [Sc in next 3 sts, 2 sc in next st] 6 times—30 sts.

RND 6: [Sc in next 4 sts, 2 sc in next st] 6 times—36 sts.

RND 7: [Sc in next 5 sts, 2 sc in next st] 6 times—42 sts.

RNDS 8–14: Sc around.

RND 15: [Sc in next 5 sts, sc2tog (see Glossary)] around—36 sts.

RND 16: [Sc in next 4 sts, sc2tog] around—30 sts.

RND 17: [Sc in next 3 sts, sc2tog] around—24 sts.

RND 18: [Sc in next 2 sts, sc2tog] around—18 sts.

Fasten off, leaving a long tail for sewing.

Face

From white felt, cut face shape, using photo as a guide. From black felt, cut 2 small "V" shapes for eyes, and a small oval for nose. Glue eyes to face and nose, centered below eyes. With black crochet thread, embroider mouth just below nose. From pink felt, cut small circles and glue to face for cheeks. Place face on head 1 rnd above last rnd (Rnd 17). With sewing needle and white thread, sew face to head. Stuff head firmly with polyester fiberfill.

Body

RNDS 1–6: Beg at bottom of body with MS, work same as Rnds 1–6 of head—36 sts.

RNDS 7–8: Sc around.

RND 9: [Sc in next 4 sts, sc2tog] 6 times—30 sts.

RND 10: Sc around.

RND 11: [Sc in next 3 sts, sc2tog] 6 times—24 sts.

RND 12: Sc around.

RND 13: [Sc in next 2 sts, sc2tog] 6 times—18 sts. Fasten off.

From white felt, cut heart-shaped chest piece. With sewing needle and white thread, sew chest piece to body, one row below top of body. Stuff body firmly.

Ears (make 2)

RNDS 1–6: With MC, work Rnds 1–6 of head—36 sts. Fasten off, leaving a long tail for sewing. Do not stuff ears.

Arms (make 2)

RND 1: With MC, ch 2, 4 sc in 2nd ch from hook—4 sts.

RND 2: 2 sc in each st around—8 sts.

RNDS 3–8: Sc around.

RND 9: Sc in next 4 sts, sl st in next st, leave rem sts unworked—4 sc.

Fasten off, leaving a long tail for sewing. Do not stuff arms.

Feet (make 2)

RNDS 1–2: With MC, work Rnds 1–2 of head—12 sts.

RNDS 3–4: Sc around.

Stuff firmly. Fasten off, leaving a long tail for sewing.

Tail

RND 1: With MC, ch 2, 6 sc in 2nd ch from hook—6 sts.

RNDS 2–7: Sc around.

RND 8: Sc in next 4 sts, sc2tog—5 sts.

RNDS 9–15: Sc around.

Do not stuff tail. Fasten off, leaving a long tail for sewing. Insert twist tie into tail until it reaches the tip. Trim off any excess tie.

Bananas (make 2)

RND 1: With CC, ch 2, 3 sc in 2nd ch from hook—3 sts.

RND 2: 2 sc in each st around—6 sts.

RNDS 3–5: Sc around.

RND 6: Sc in next 4 sts, sc2tog—5 sts.

RNDS 7–8: Sc around.

Fasten off, leaving a long tail for sewing. Do not stuff bananas. Sew bananas tog at open ends. From brown felt, cut a small circle for stem. Glue stem over top of bananas.

Finishing

Note: Use long tails to sew pieces tog. Sew head to body. Make sure heart-shaped chest piece is centered directly below face. For ears, fold circles in half to create semicircles. Sew ears to sides of head in a cuplike formation. From white felt, cut 2 semicircle shapes for inner ear pieces. Glue these pieces inside ears. Position arms in an embracing position. Sew arms in place. Sew hands tog to secure. Position feet facing outward from body, ensuring that placement will allow monkey to sit on its own. Sew feet to body. Sew tail to back end of body. Curl tail to your liking once it is sewn in place. Position bananas anywhere you think is most charming, even on the monkey's tail. Sew bananas in place. 🖉

JOANNA MA first started crocheting at age eight for a class elective in Chinese School and was told that she had no talent, so she gave up. Seventeen years later, she picked up crochet again just for fun and her creative juices haven't stopped since!

Finished Size
About 6" (15 cm) tall when sitting.

Yarn
Red Heart Super Saver (100% acrylic; 364 yd [333 m]/7 oz [198 g]; (**4**)): #0311 white (MC), 2 oz; #0324 bright yellow (CC2), about 1 oz; #126 chocolate (CC3), less than 1 oz. Yarn distributed by Coats & Clark.

Lily Sugar'n Cream Super Size (100% cotton; 150 yd [138 m]/3 oz [85 g]; (**4**)): #19605 creamsicle (CC1), about 2 oz.

Hook
Sizes G/6 (4 mm) and H/8 (5 mm). Adjust hook size if necessary to obtain correct gauge.

Notions
St markers (m); yarn needle; pair of 18 mm safety eyes; polyester fiberfill.

Gauge
10 sts and 10 rows = 2" (5 cm) in sc with smaller hook. Gauge is not critical for this project.

- -

notes

* Exact gauge is not necessary for this project. Gauge should be tight enough to make a fabric that will hold the stuffing in place and keep its shape.

* Most pieces are worked in spirals. Do not join rnds. Use st marker (m) to indicate beg of rnd, move m up as each rnd is completed.

* To change color, work last st of old color to last yo. Yo with new color and draw through all lps on hook. Proceed with new color. Fasten off old color.

- -

stitch guide

Beaded single crochet (bsc)
Insert hook in indicated st and pull up lp, slide button up close to hook, yo and draw through both lps on hook. Keep button on RS of piece as work progresses.

- -

Sunny the Bunny
by Laura Gibbons

Sunny adores playing in fields of sunflowers. She loves sunflowers so much that wears she them on her dress, and if she finds one big enough, she will wear one on her head as well. She is a shy girl but will warm your heart with her smile.

Head

RND 1: With MC and smaller hook, make an adjustable lp (see Glossary), 7 sc in ring—7 sc.

RND 2: 2 sc in each sc around—14 sc.

RND 3: [Sc in next sc, 2 sc in next sc] 7 times—21 sc.

RND 4: [Sc in next 2 sc, 2 sc in next sc] 7 times—28 sc.

RND 5: [Sc in next 3 sc, 2 sc in next sc] 7 times—35 sc.